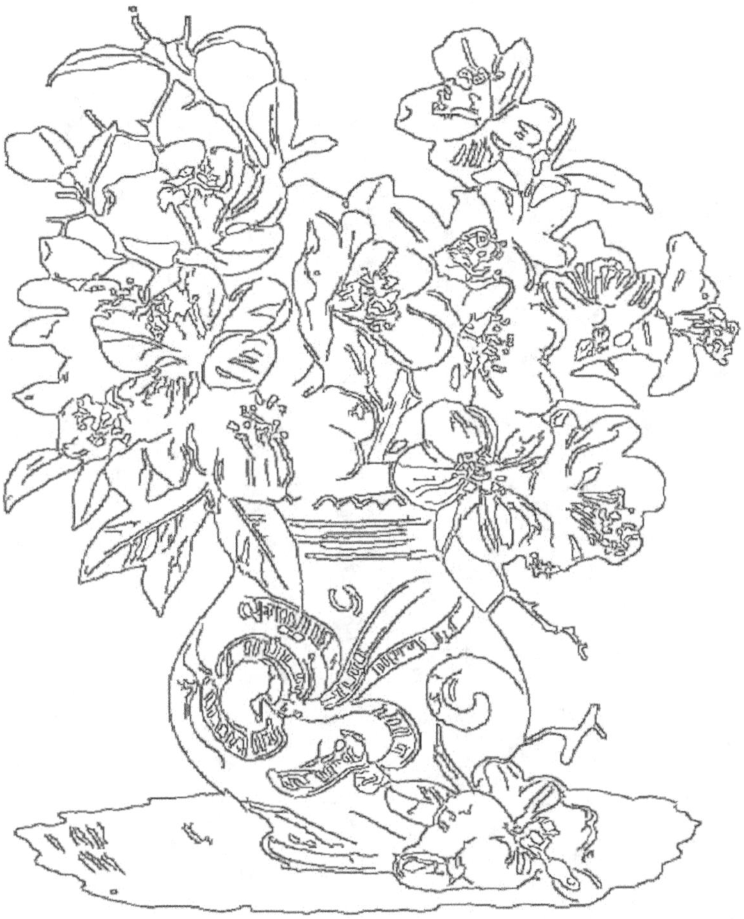

Enjoy Coloring !!!

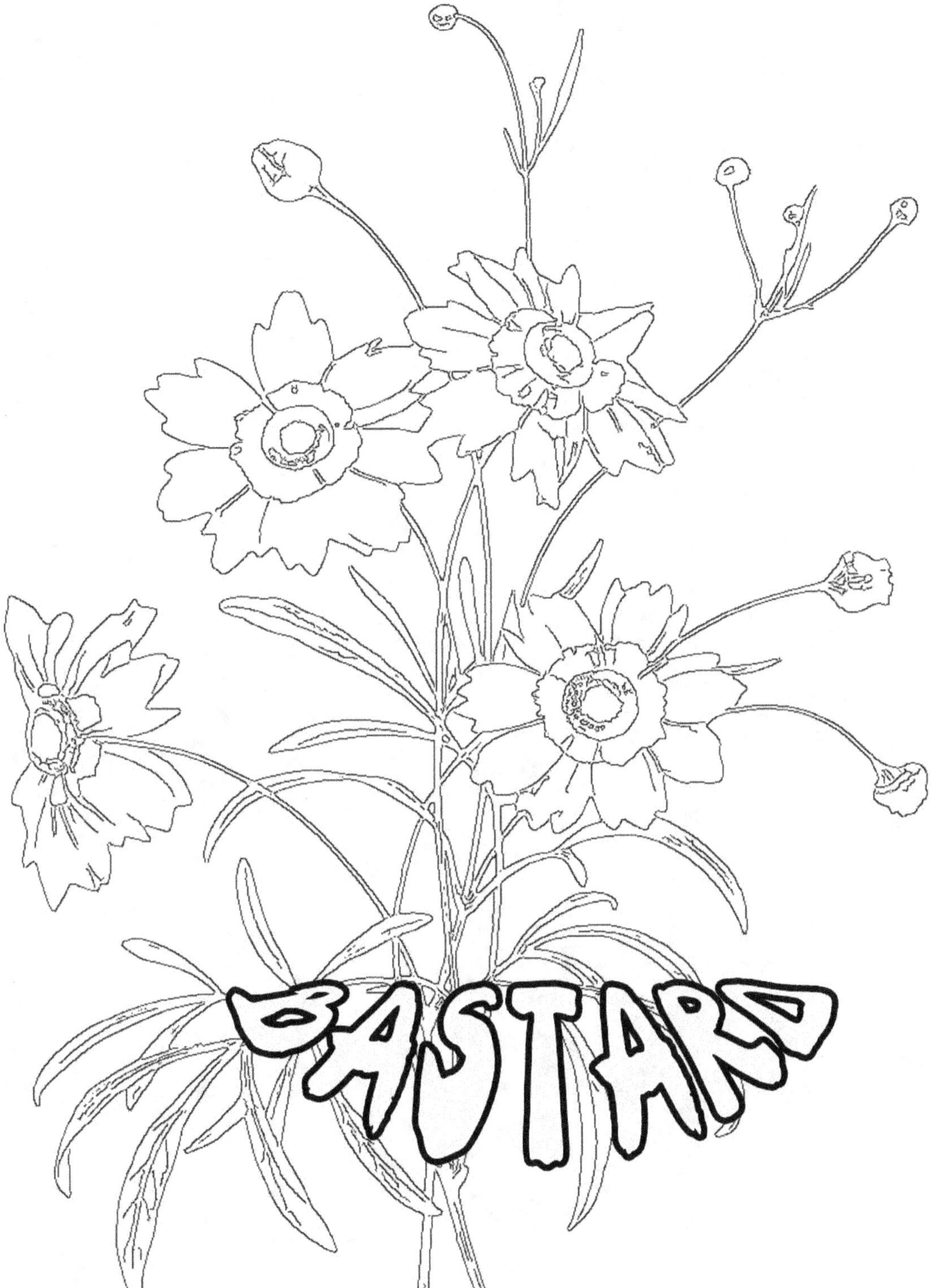
BASTARD

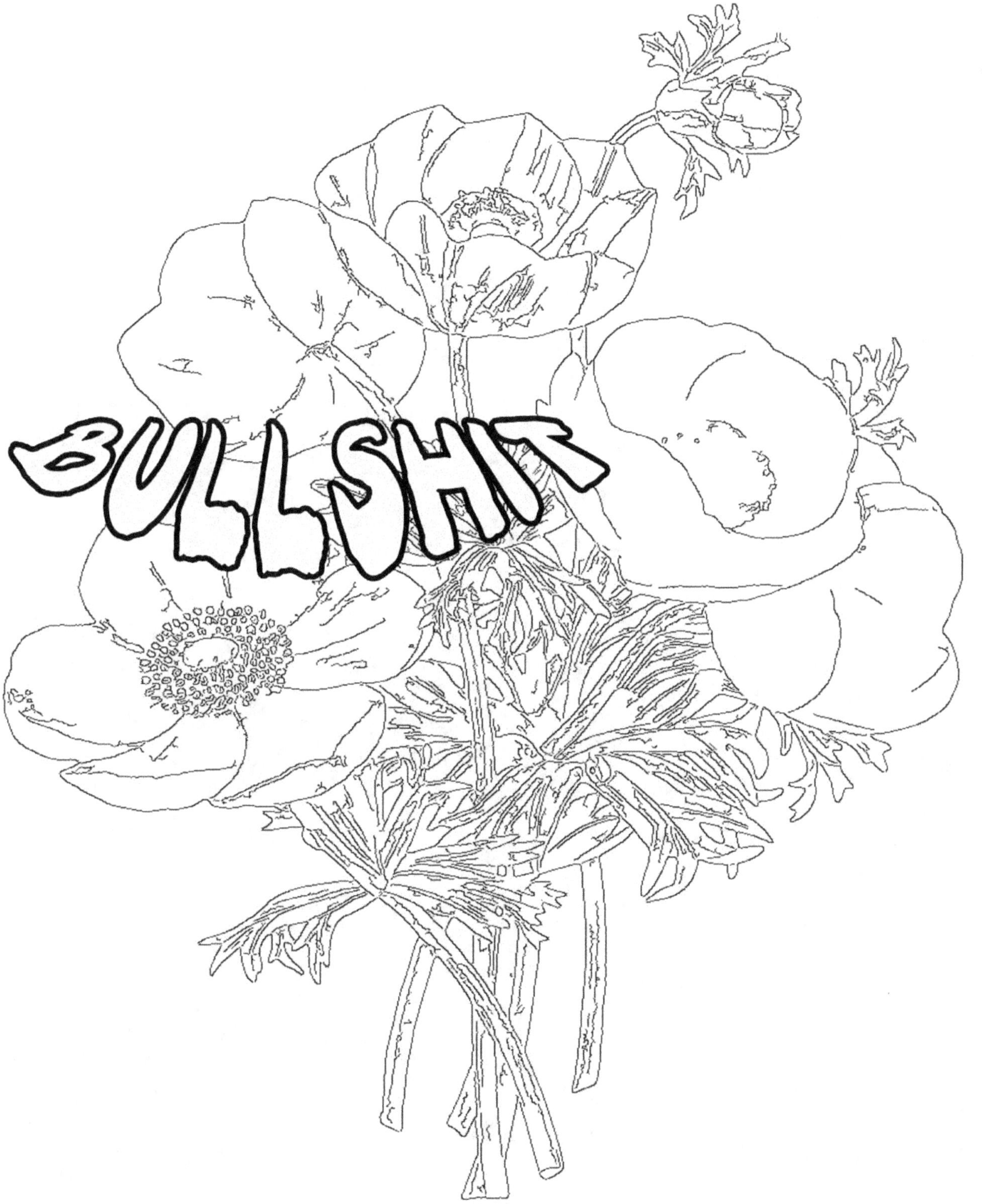
BULLSHIT

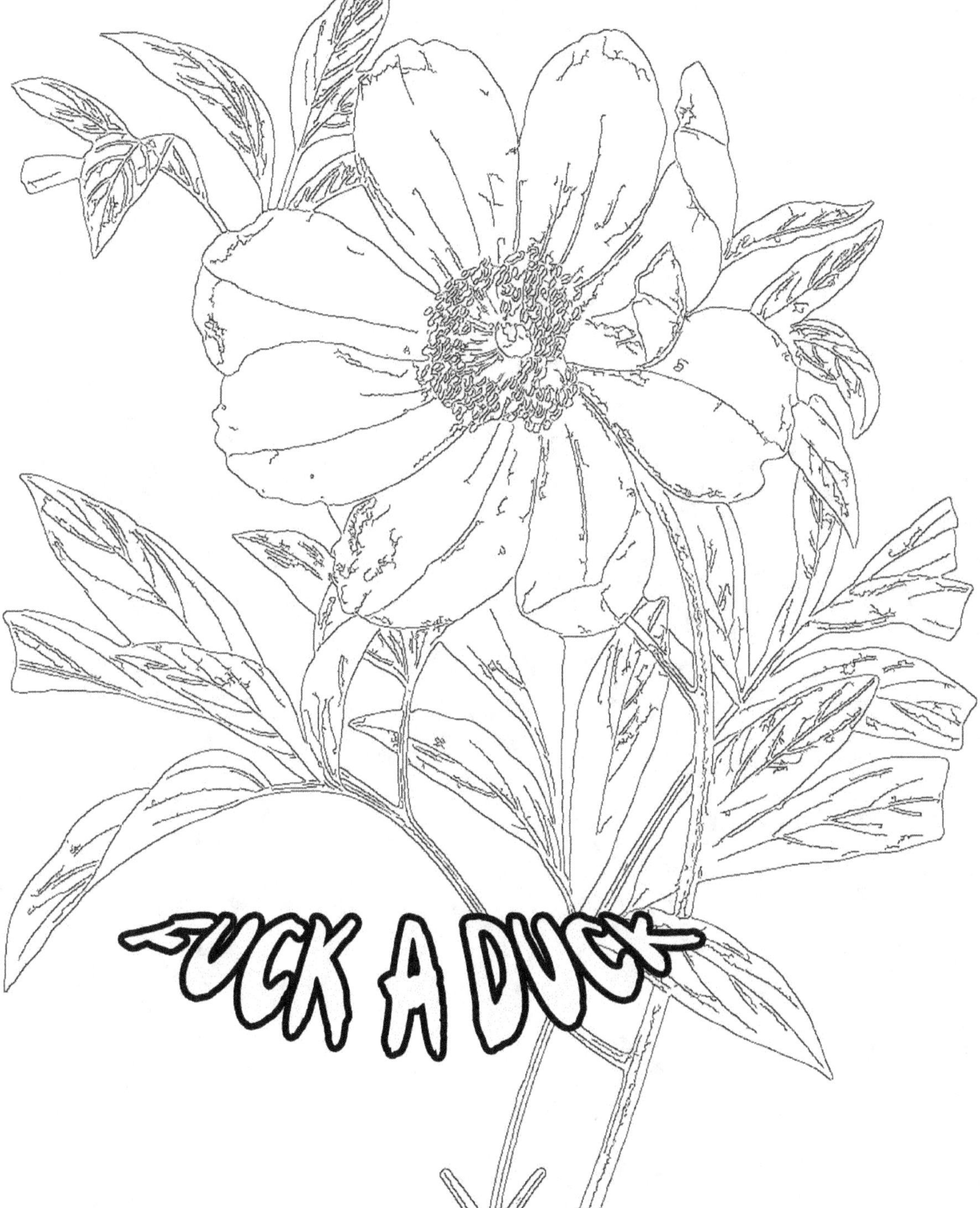
FUCK A DUCK

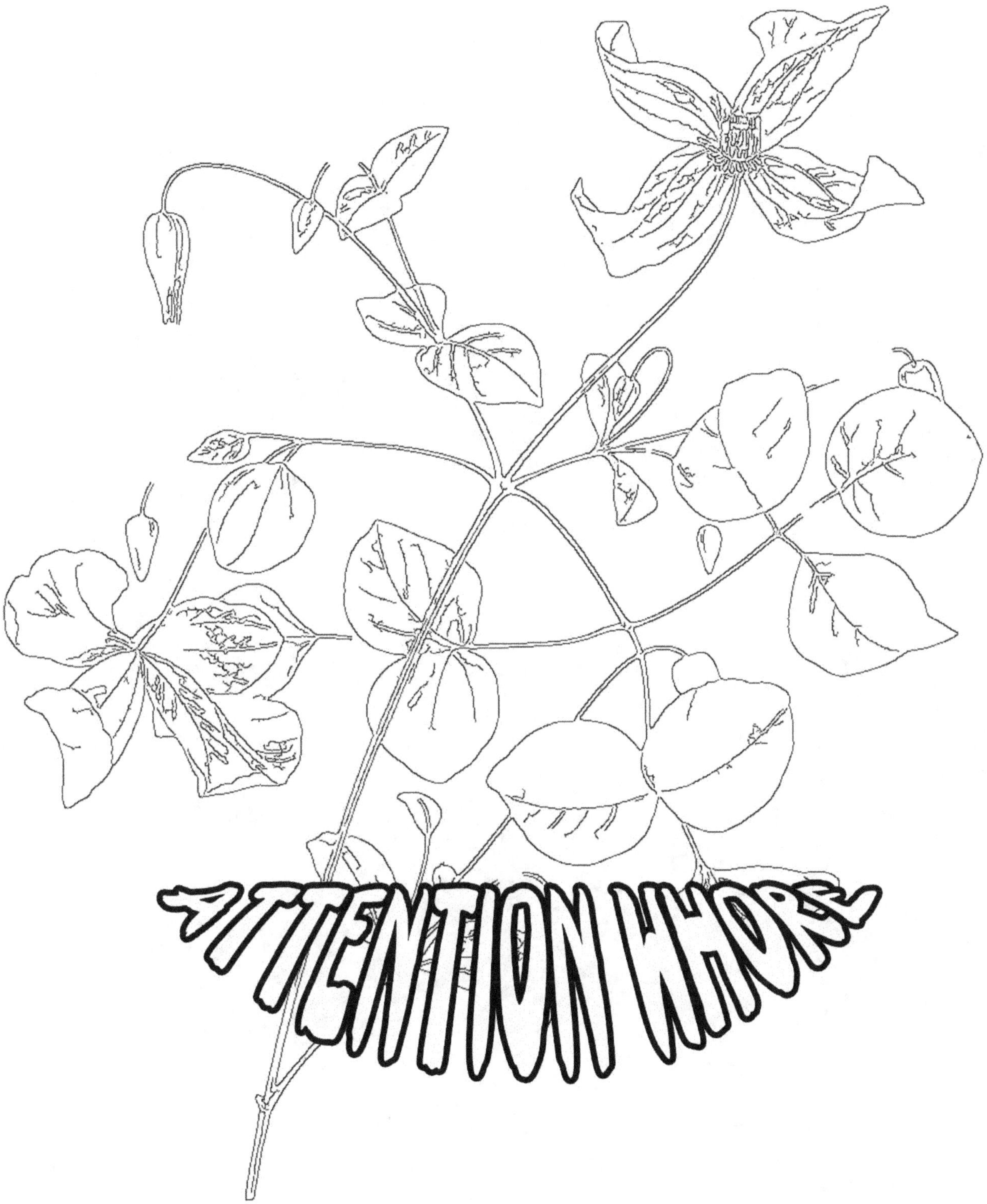
ATTENTION WHORE

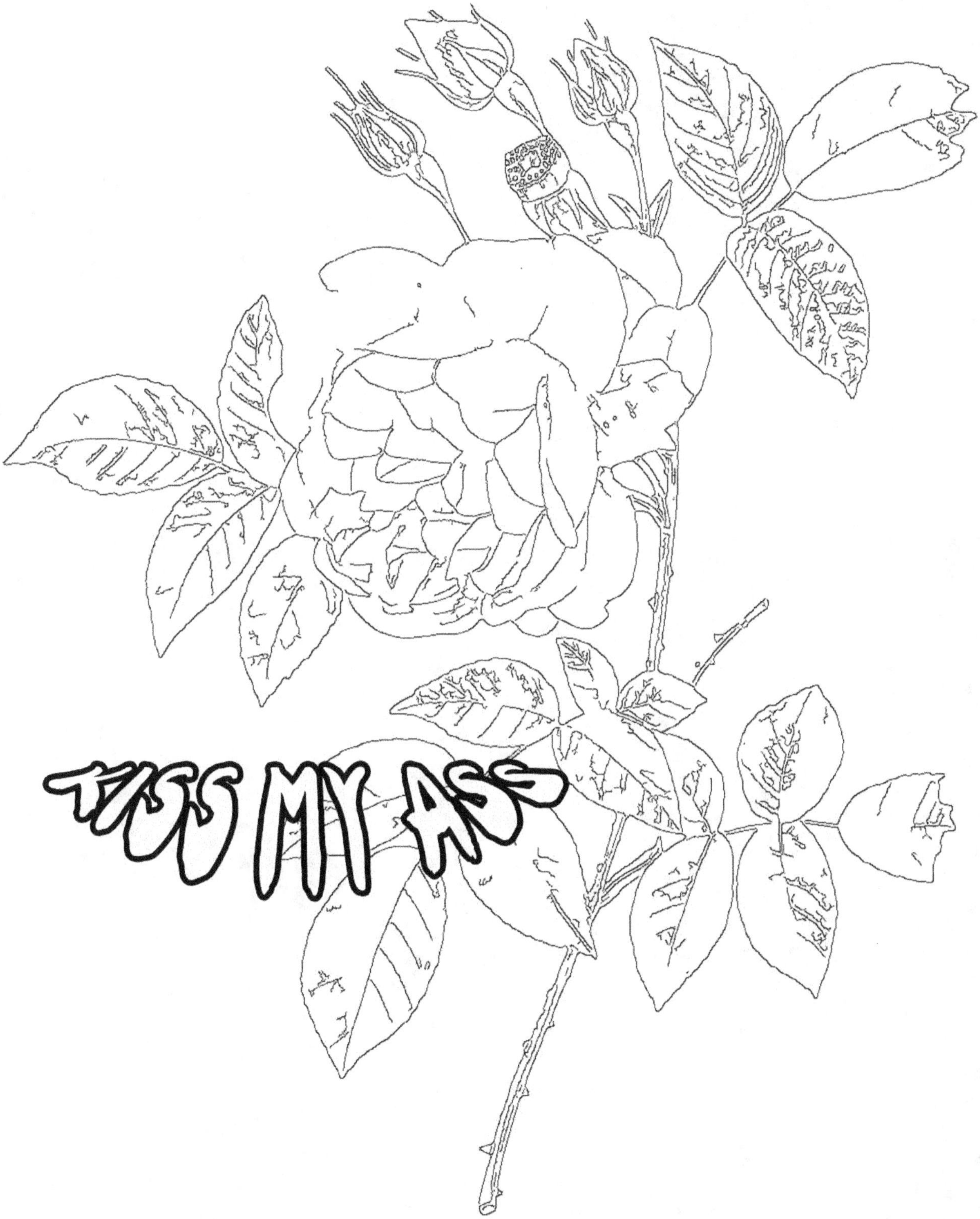
KISS MY ASS

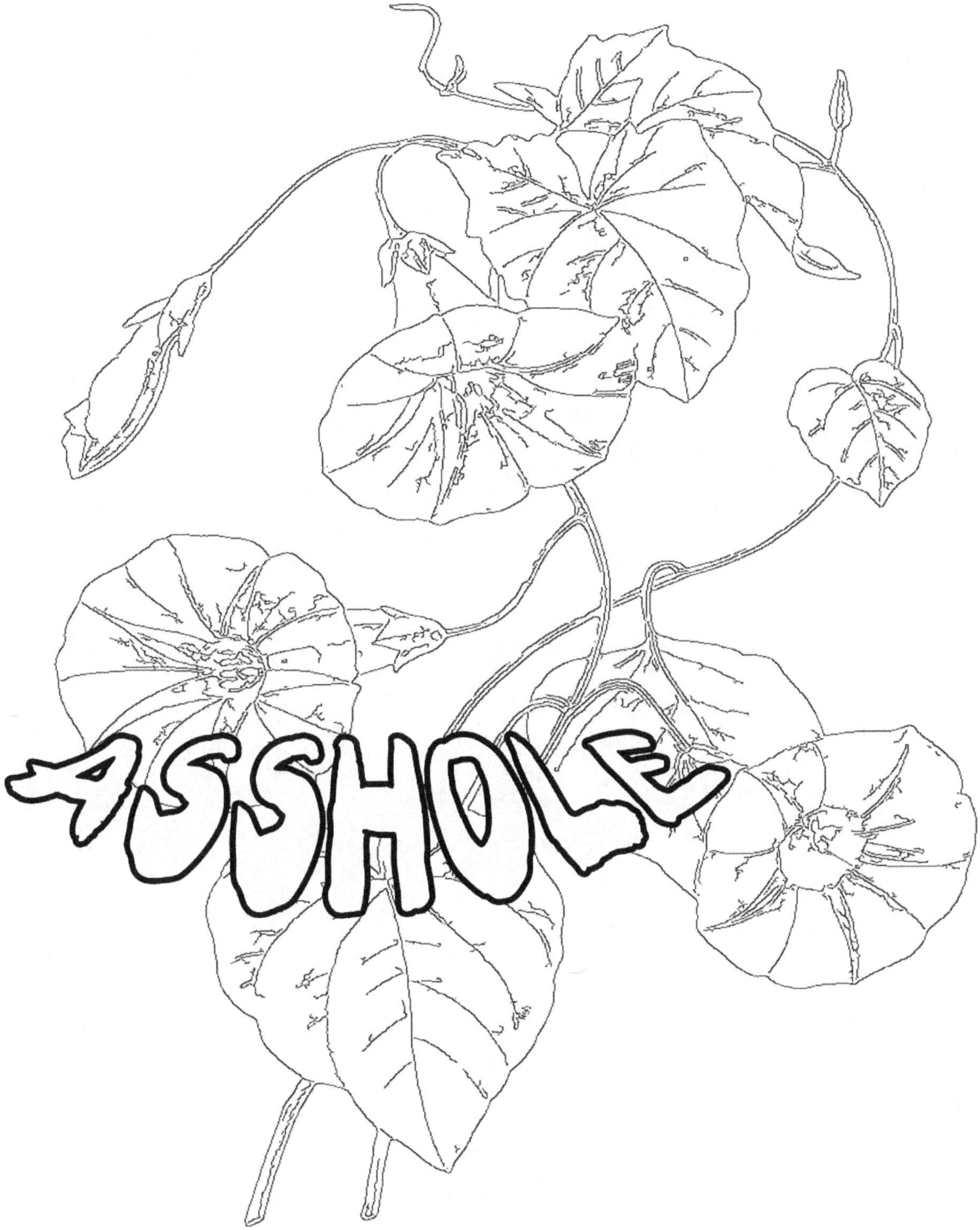
ASSHOLE

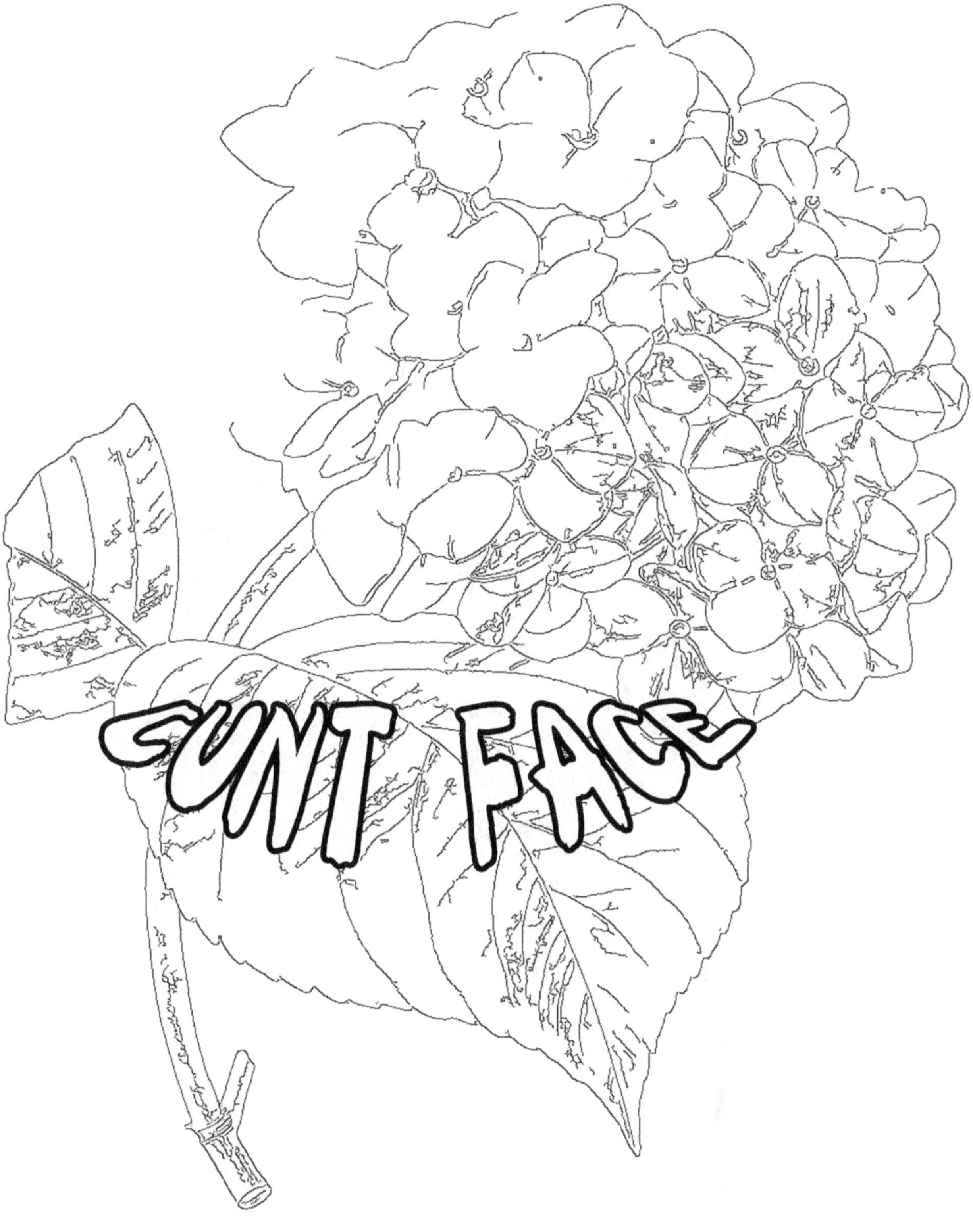
CUNT FACE

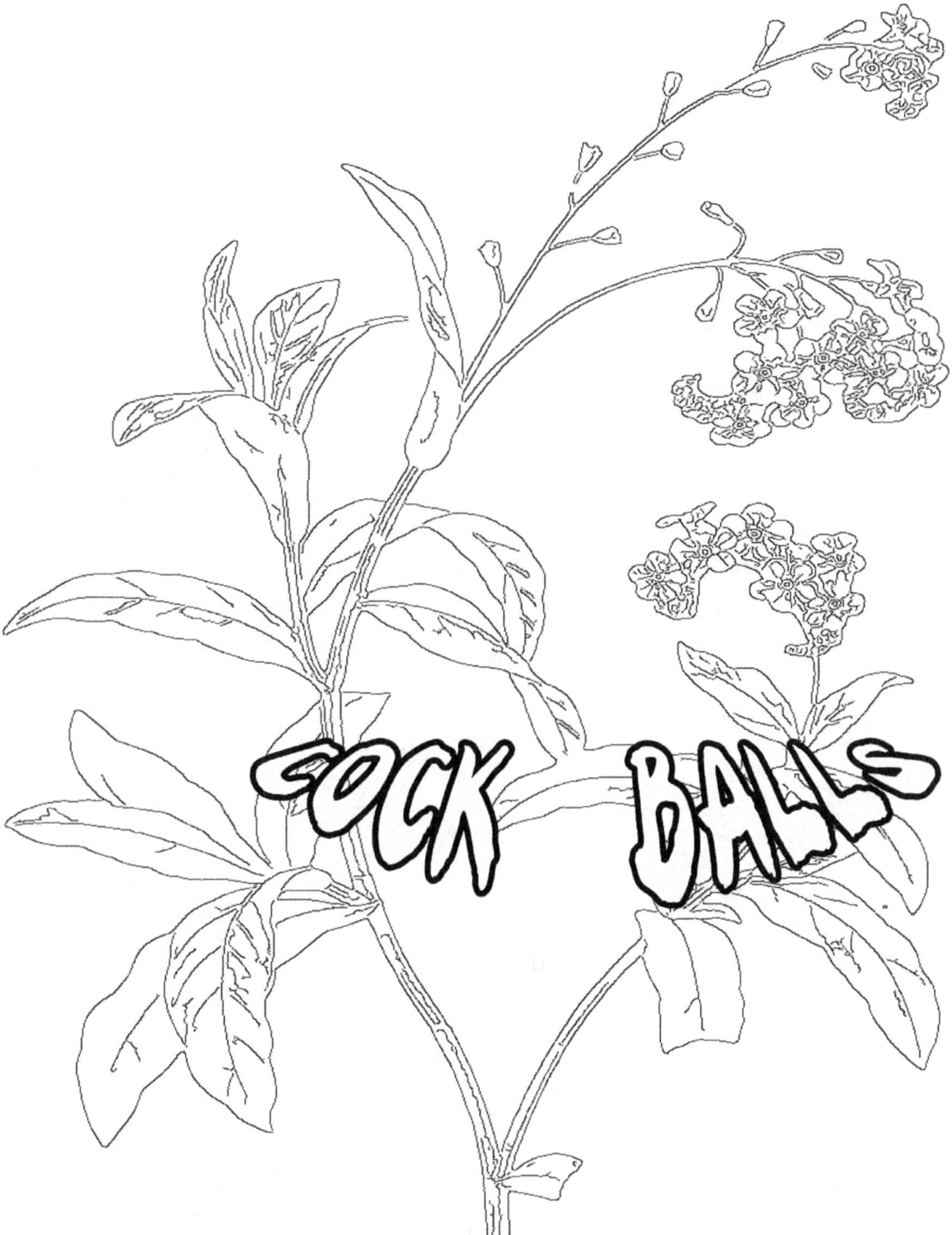
COCK BALLS

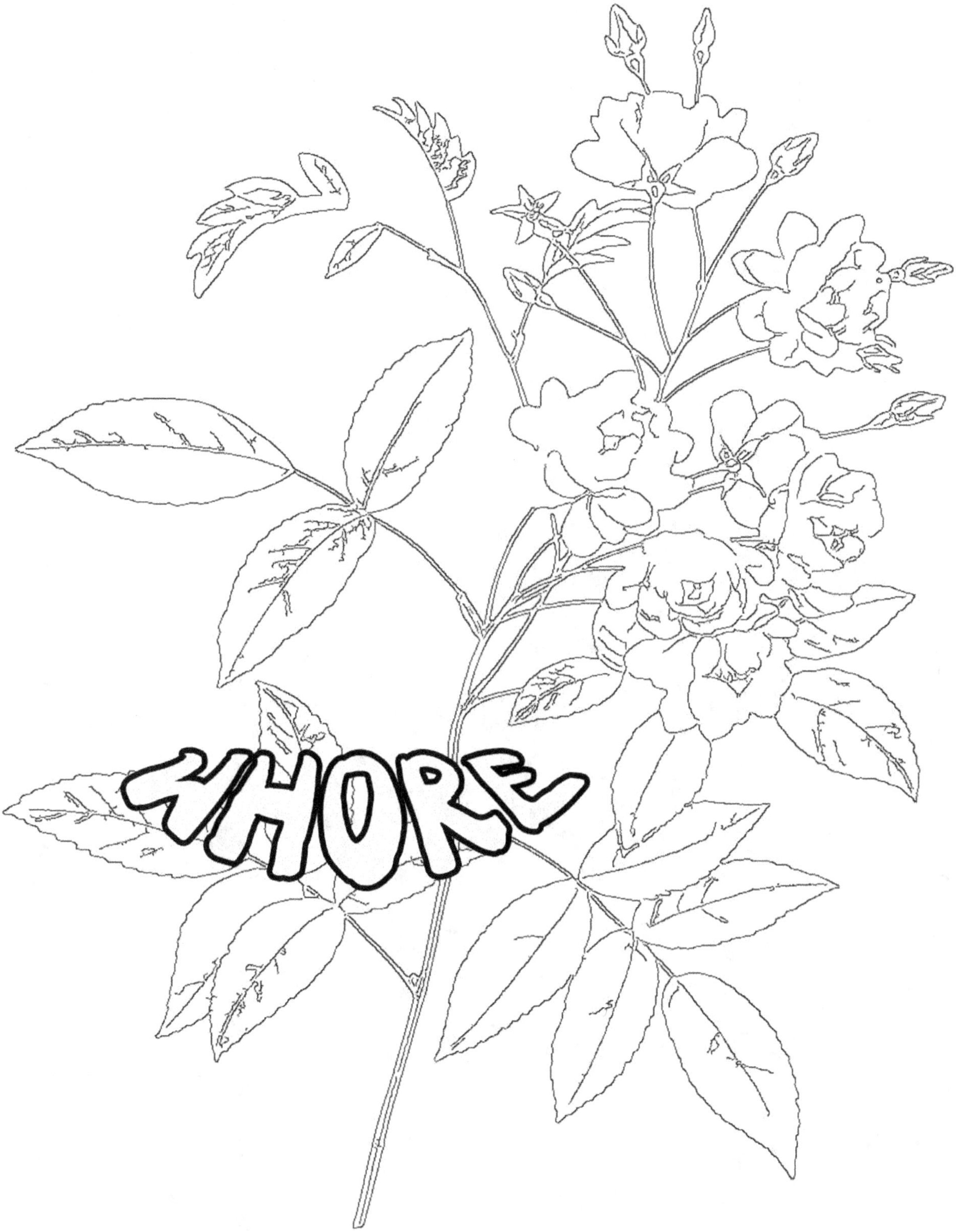
WHORE

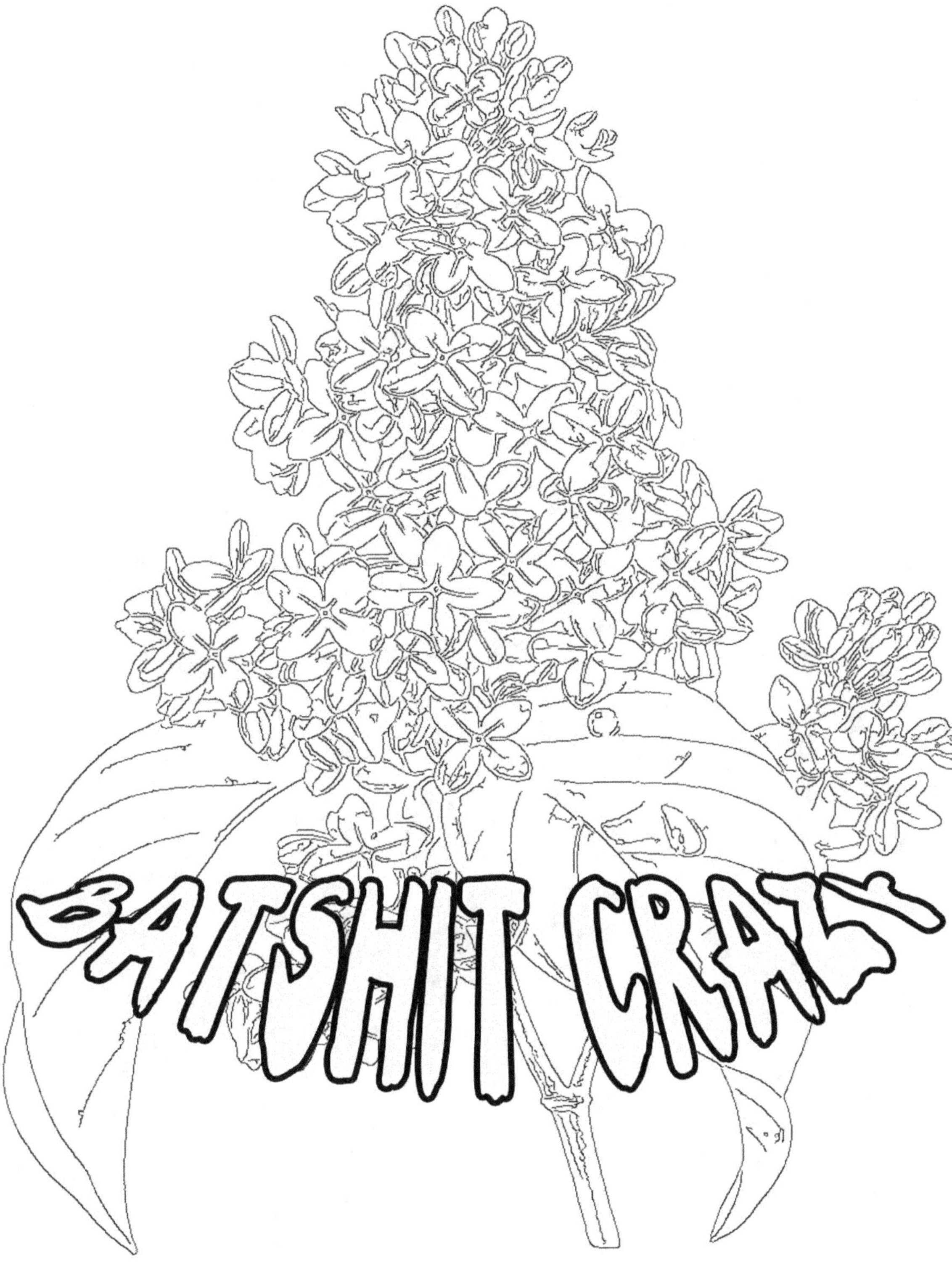
BATSHIT CRAZY

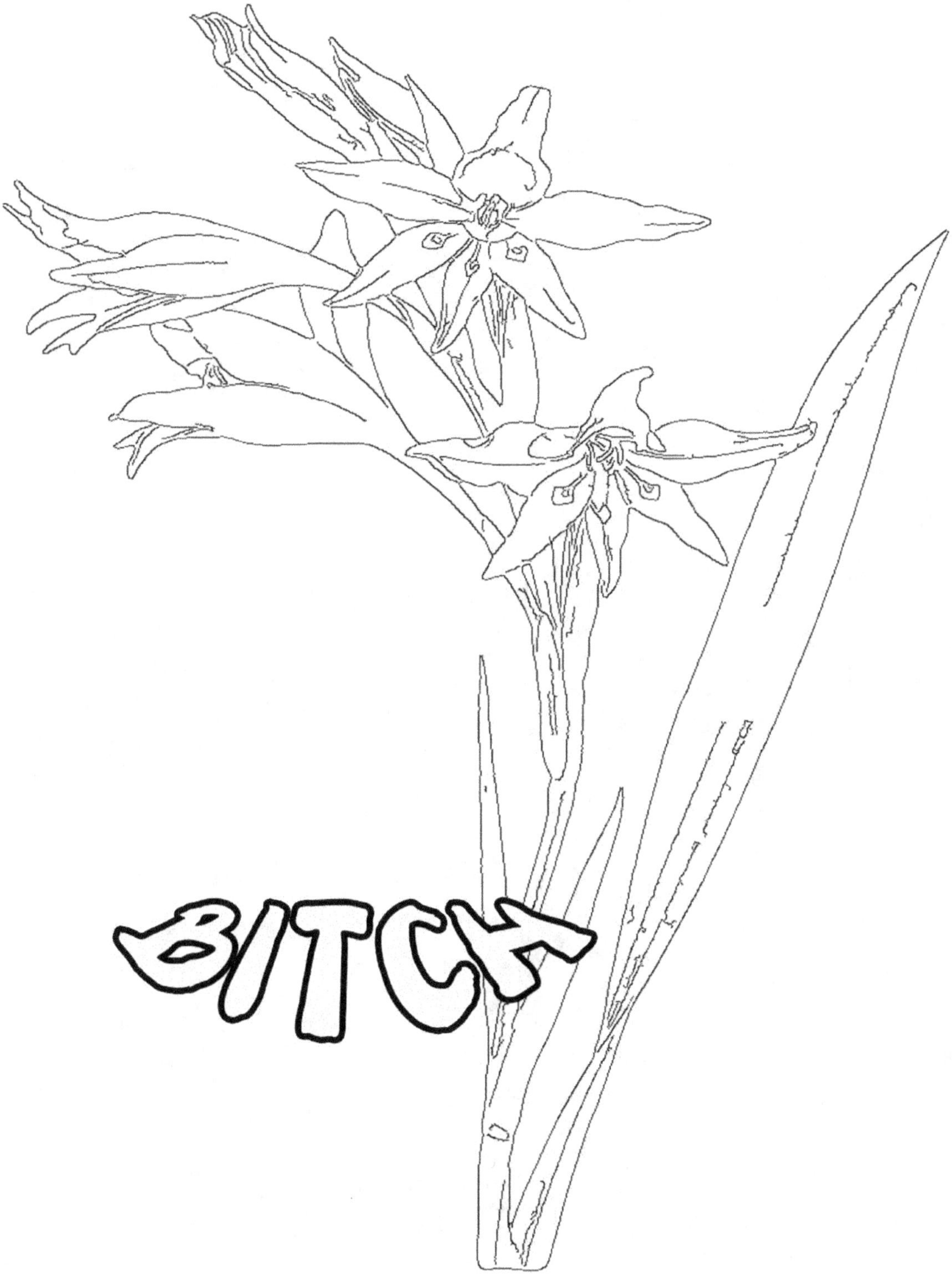
BITCH

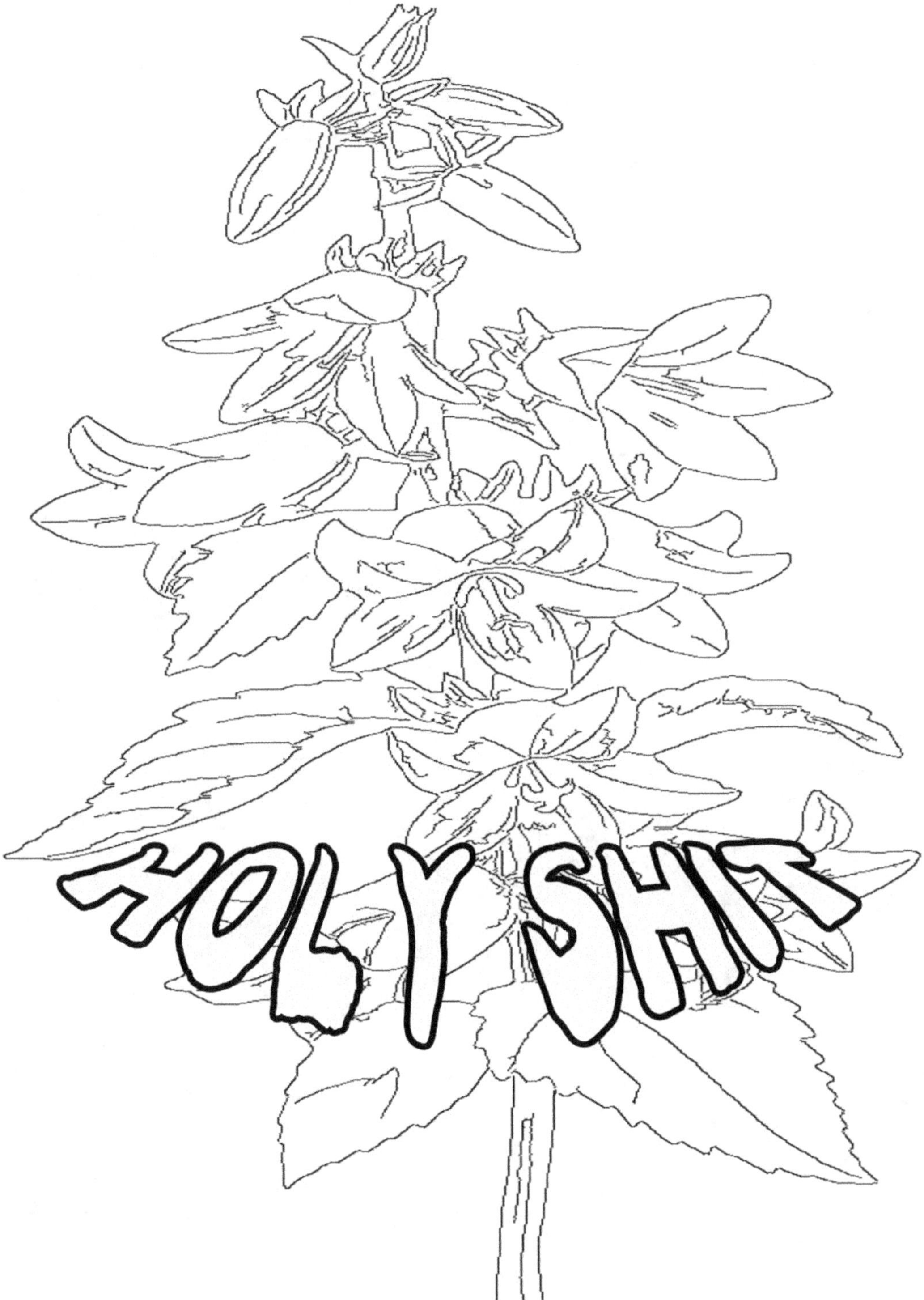
HOLY SHIT

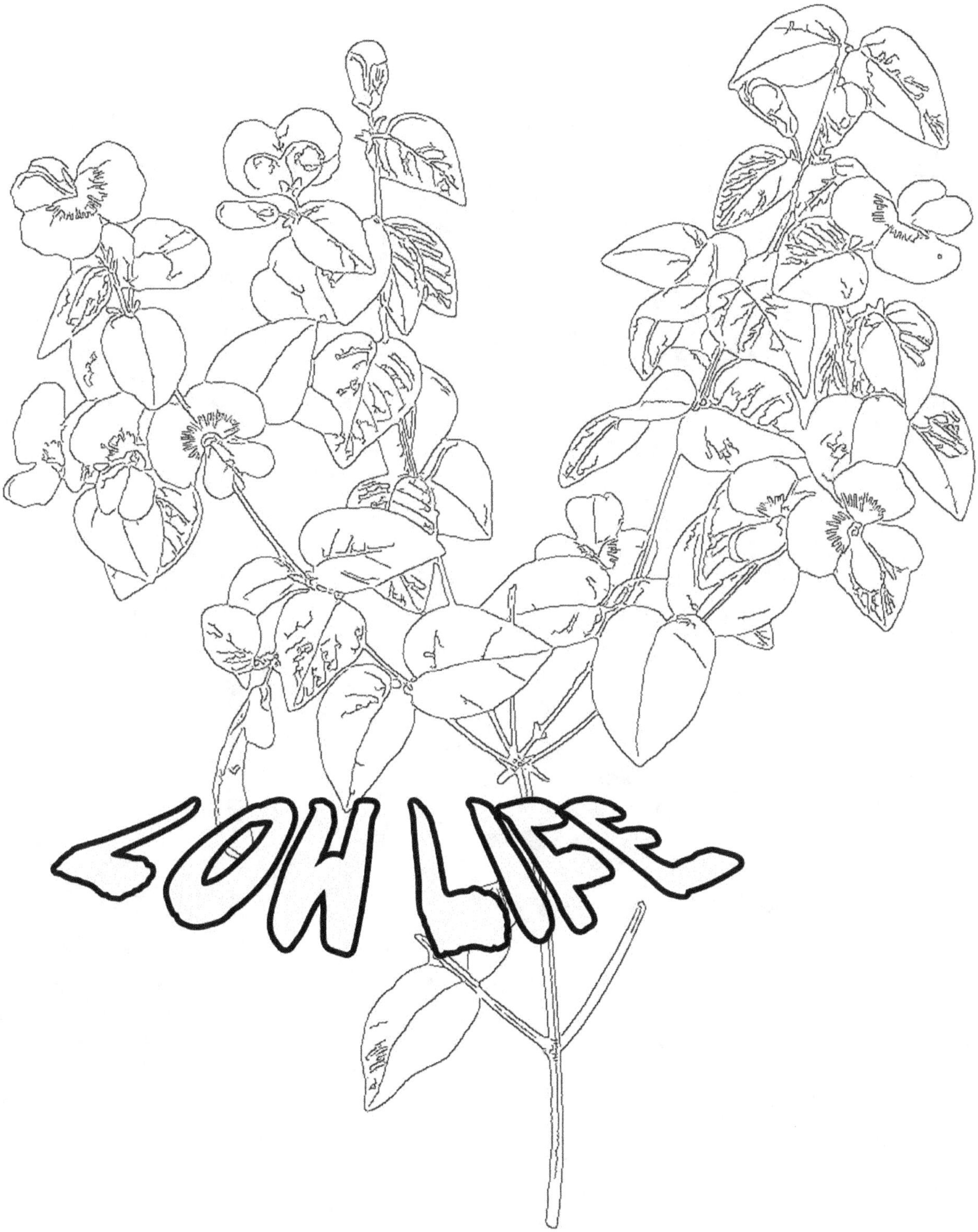
LOW LIFE

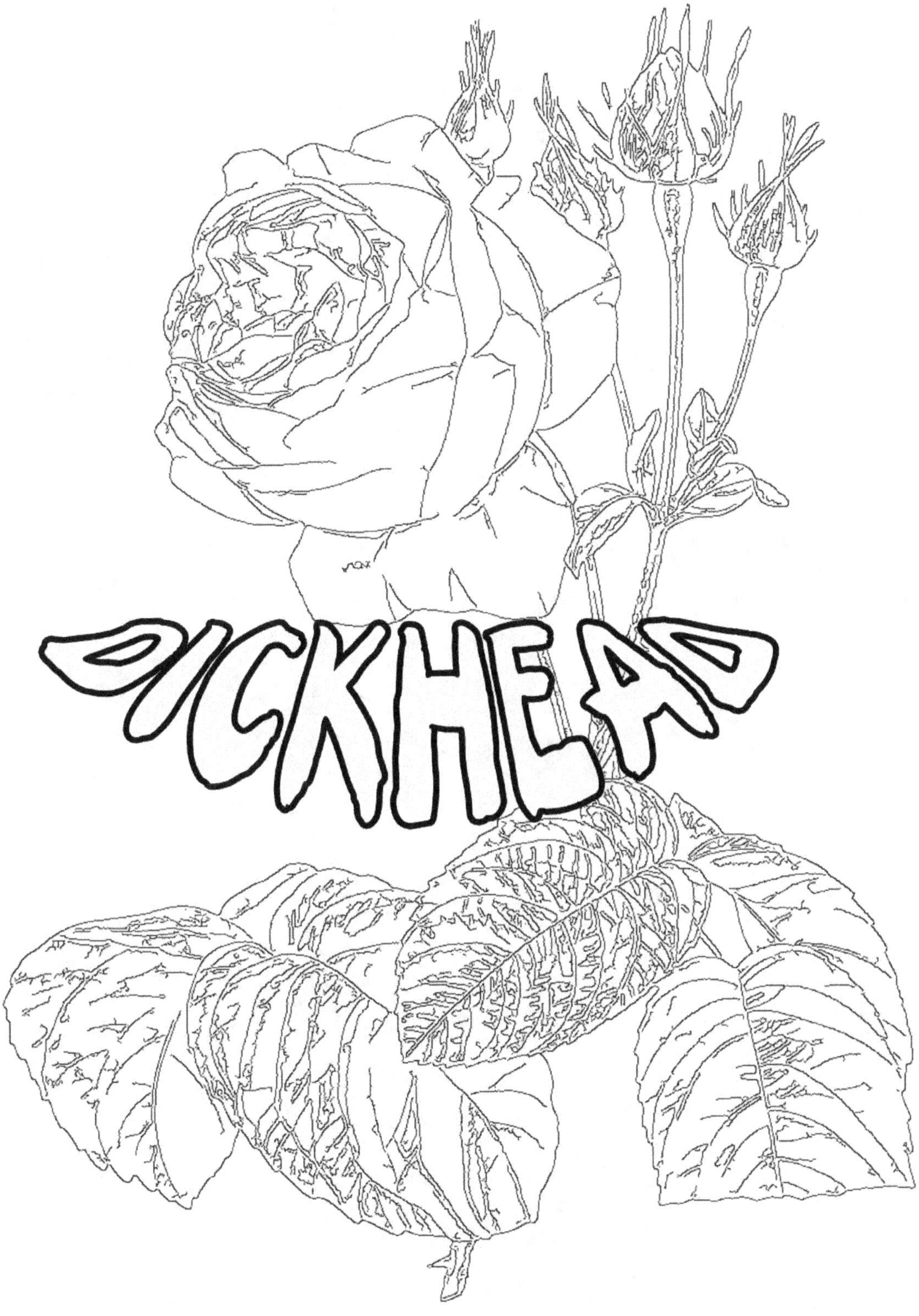
DICKHEAD

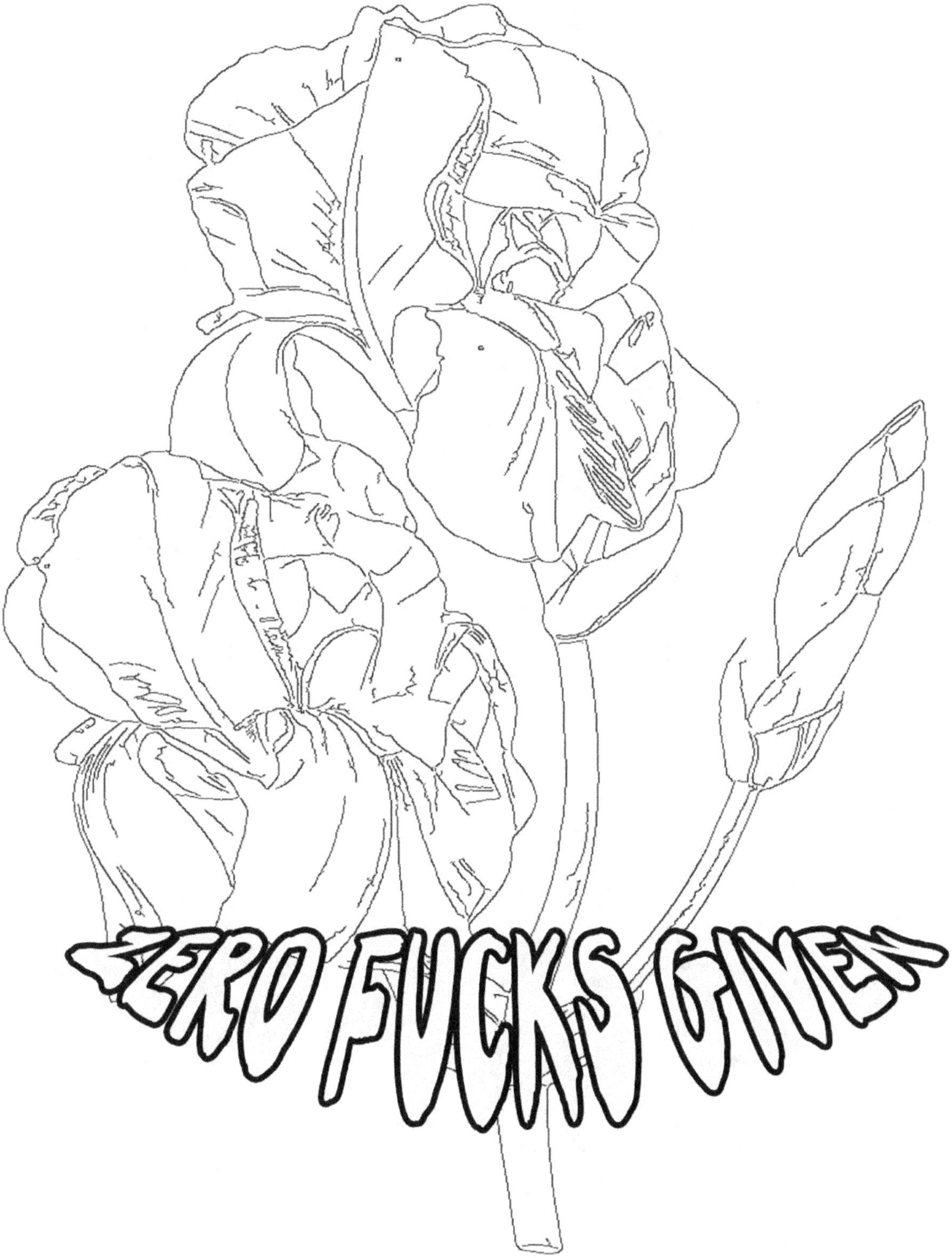
ZERO FUCKS GIVEN

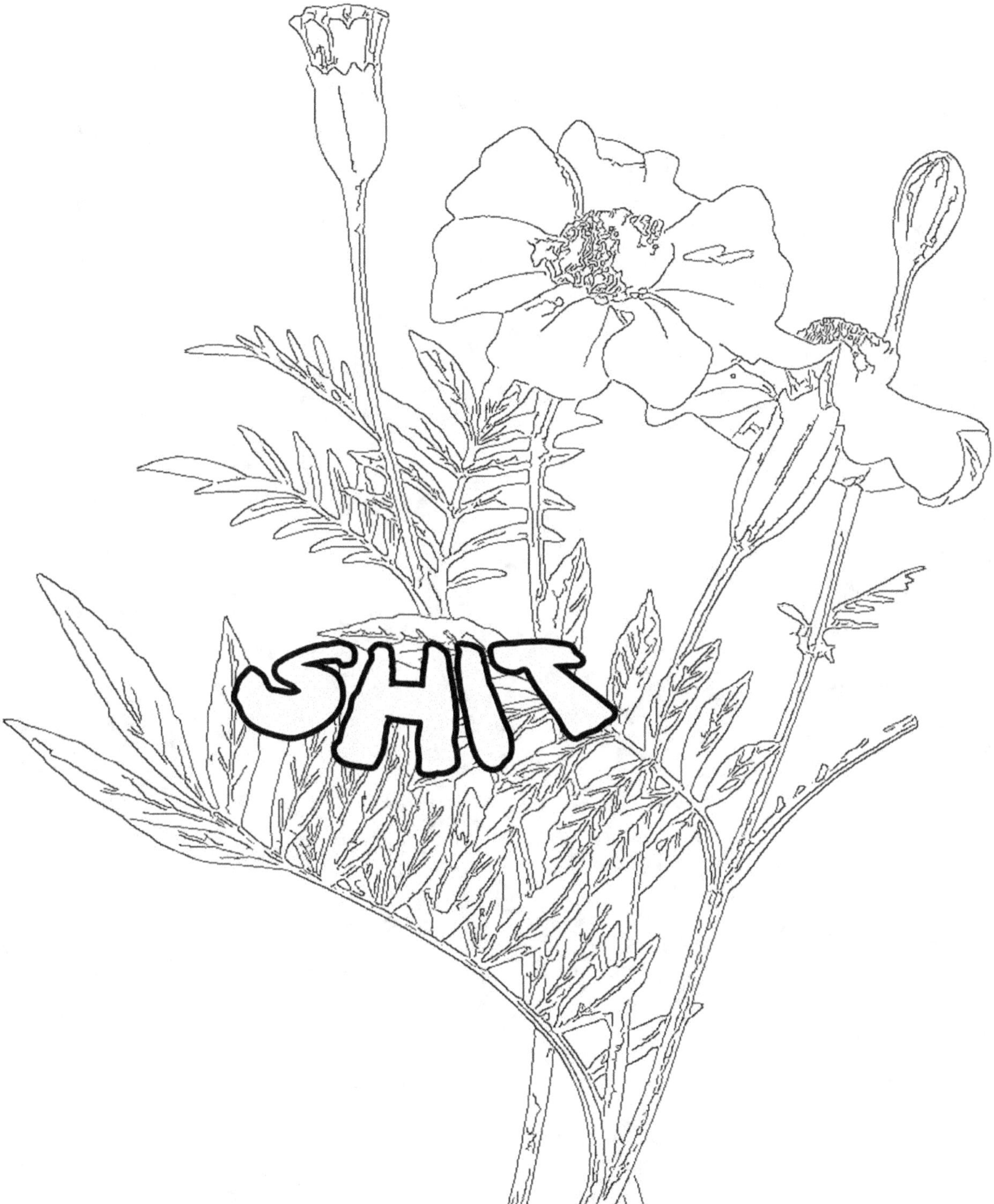
SHIT

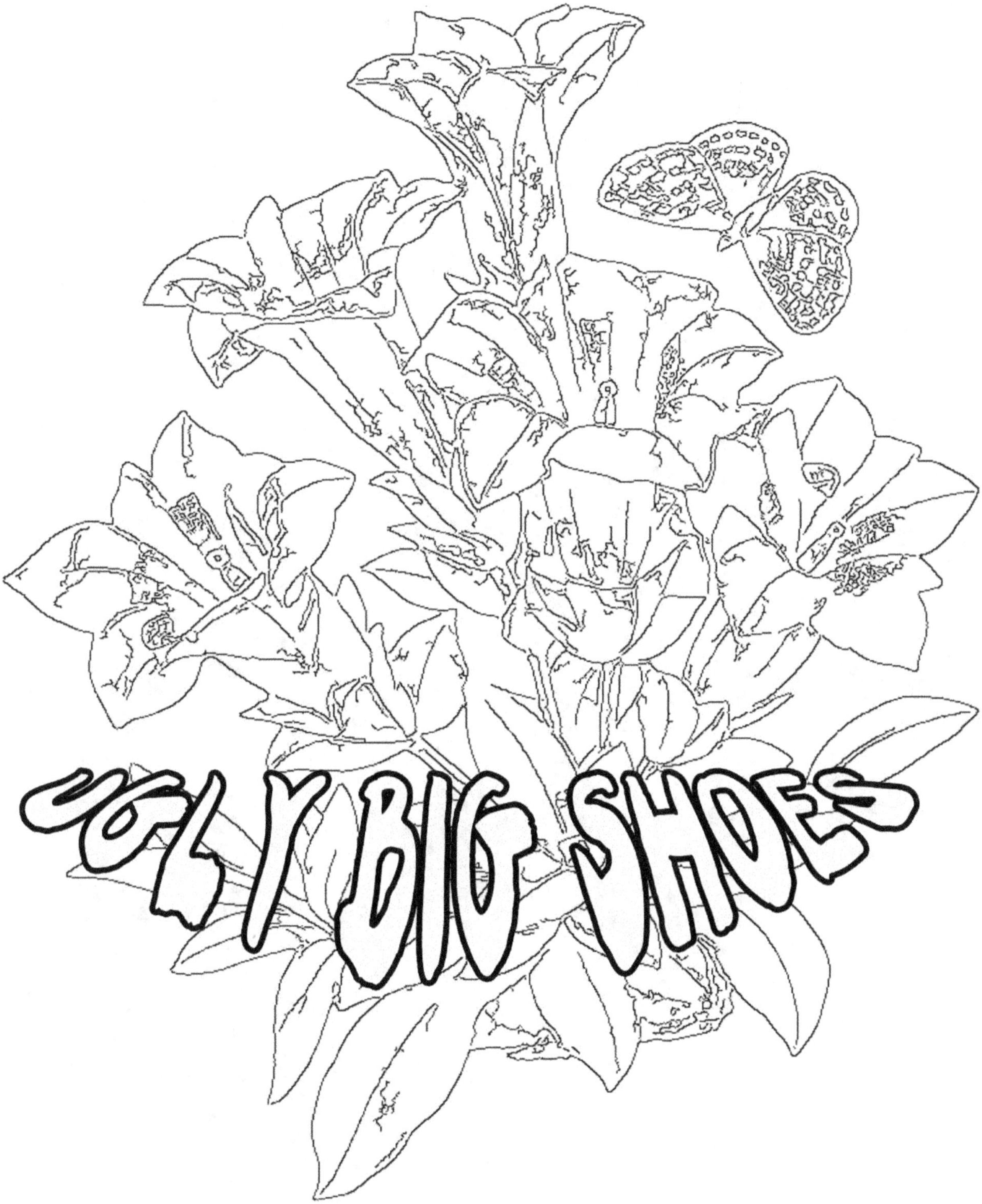
UGLY BIG SHOES

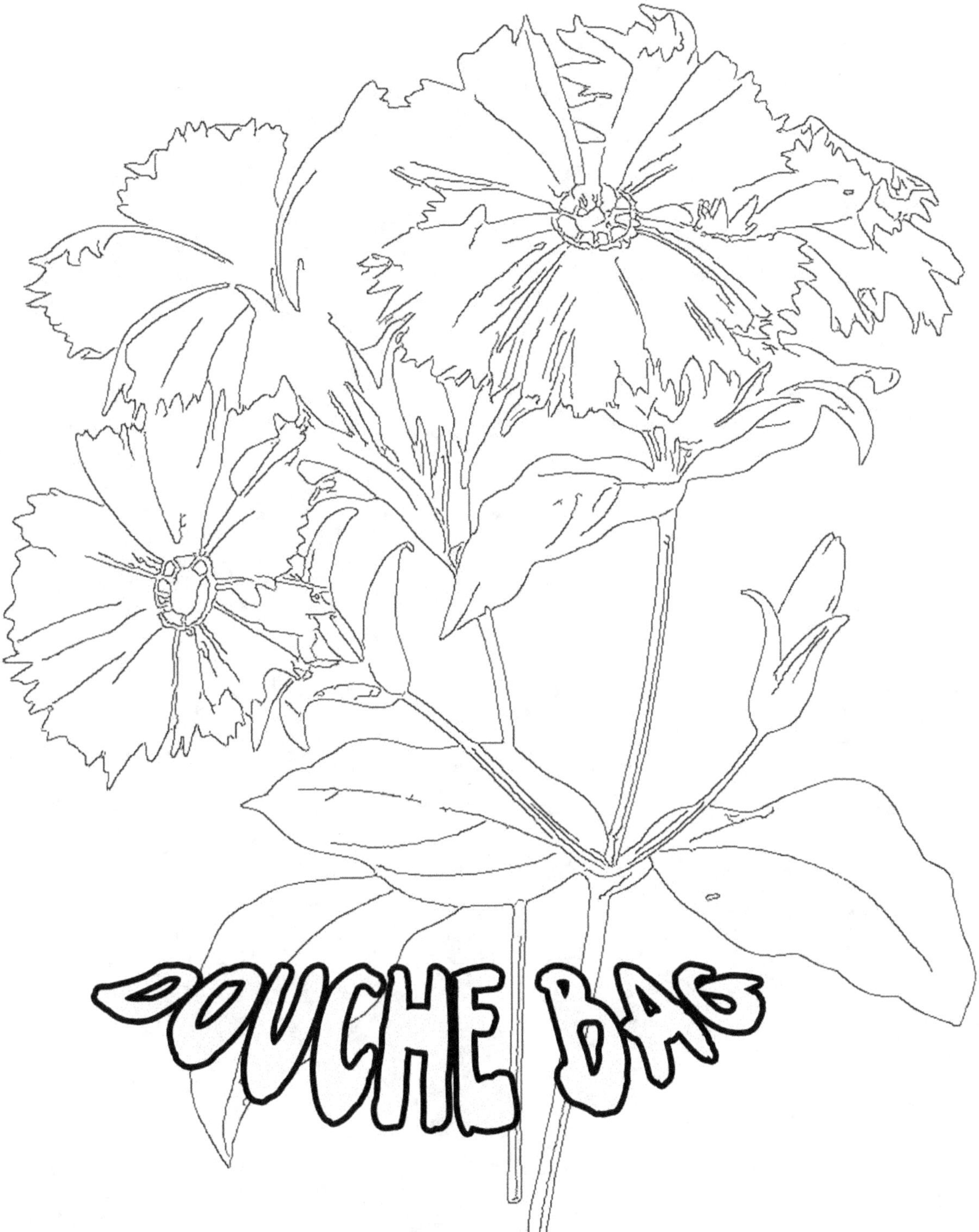
DOUCHE BAG

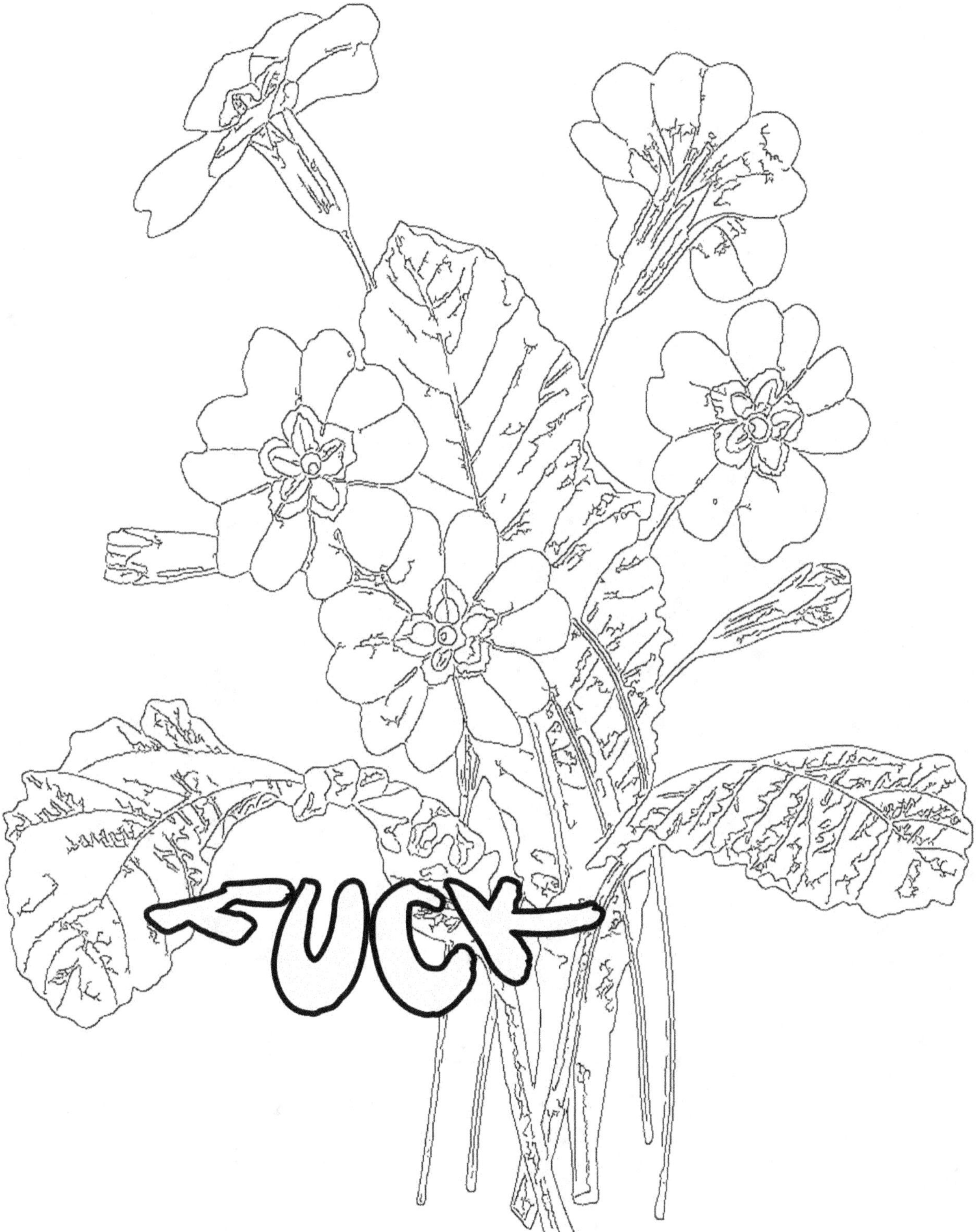
FUCK

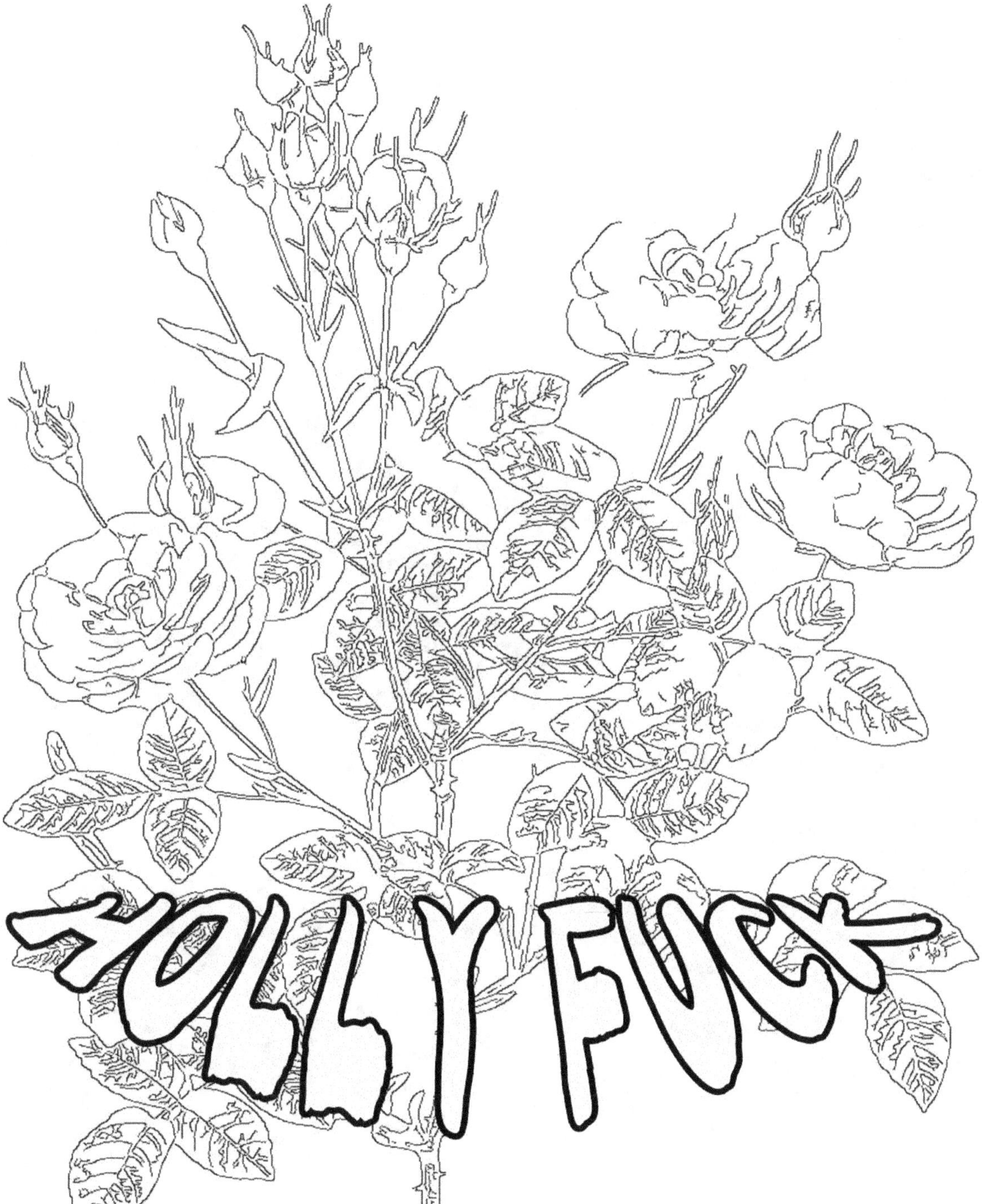
HOLLY FUCK

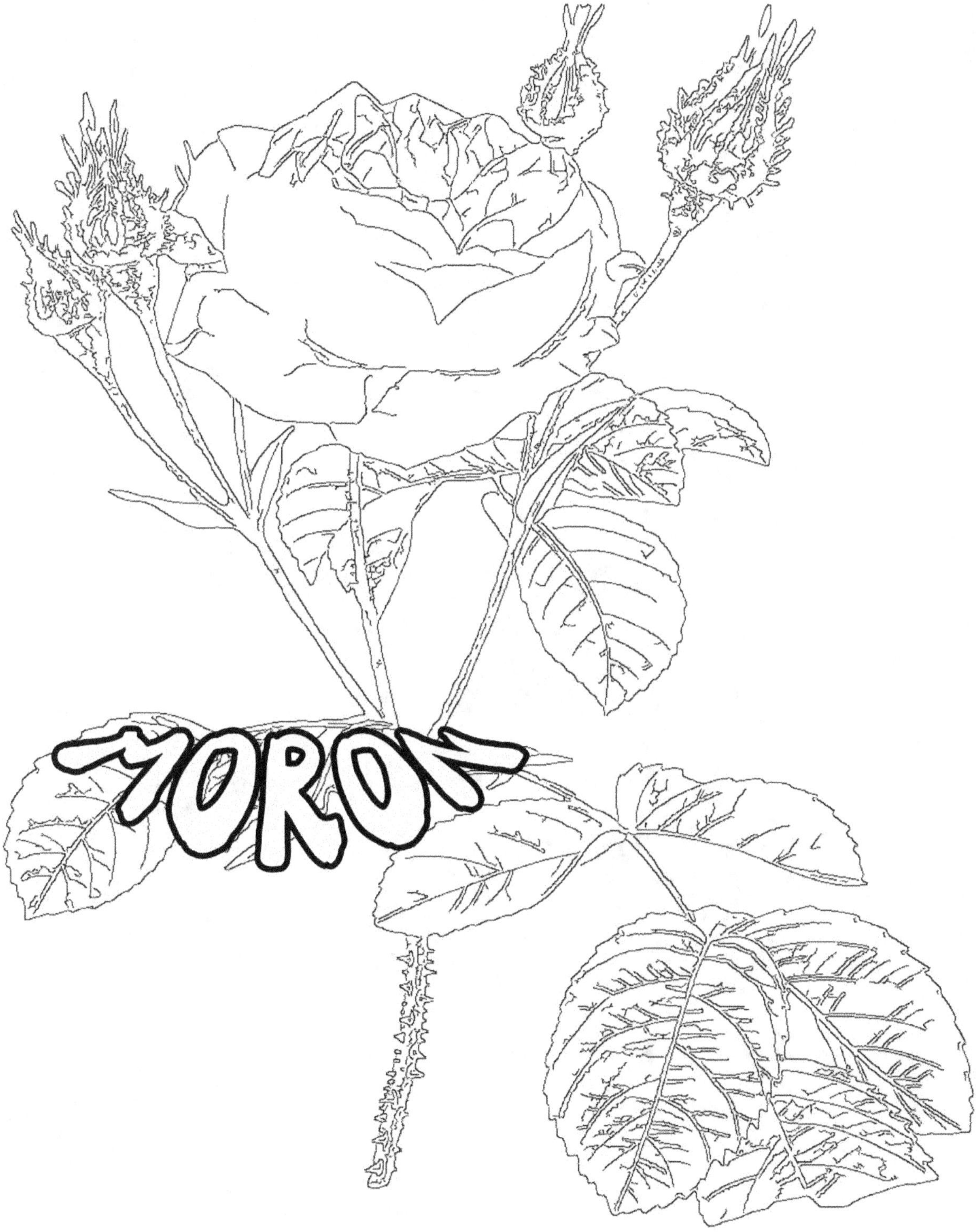
MORON

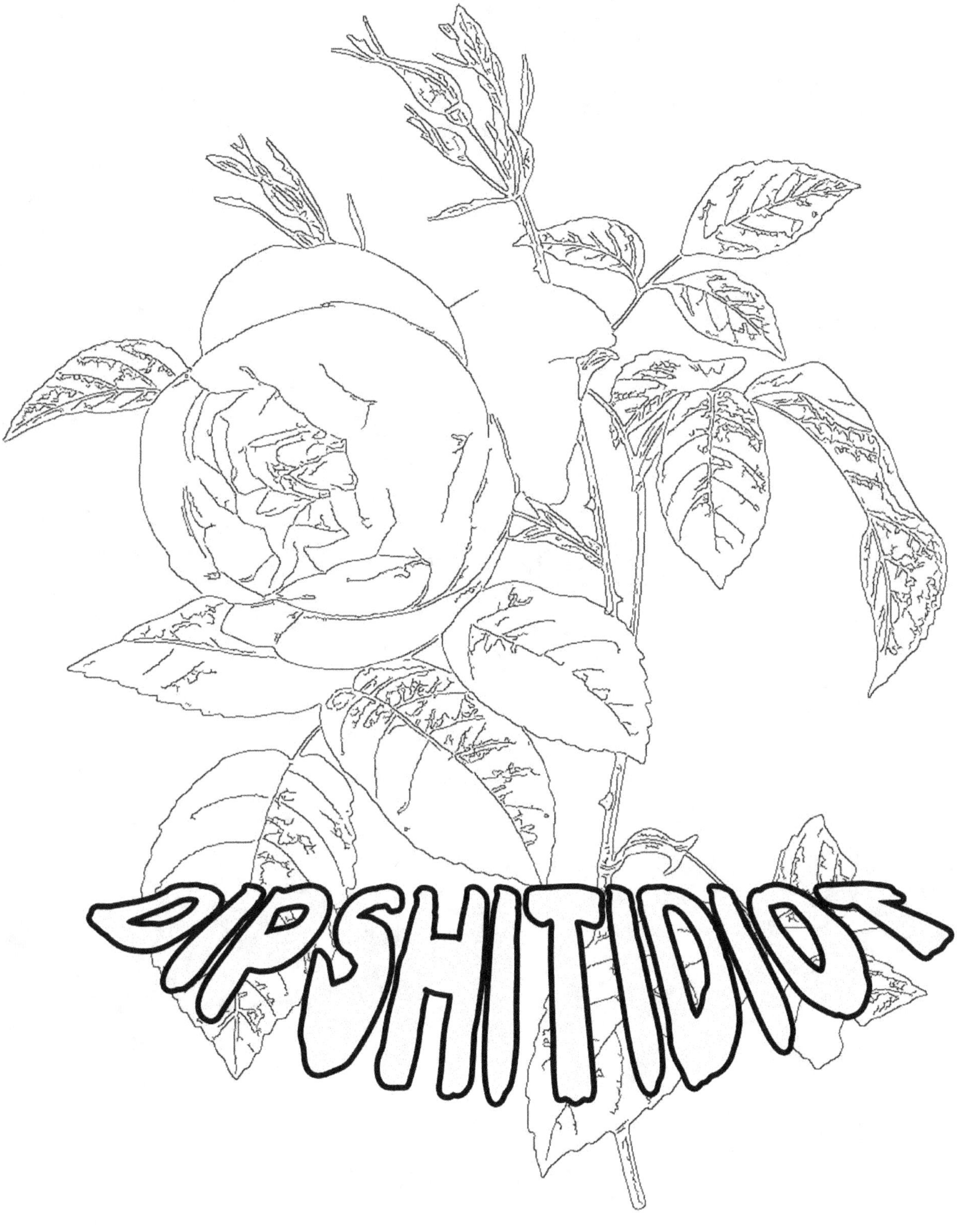
DIPSHITIDIOT

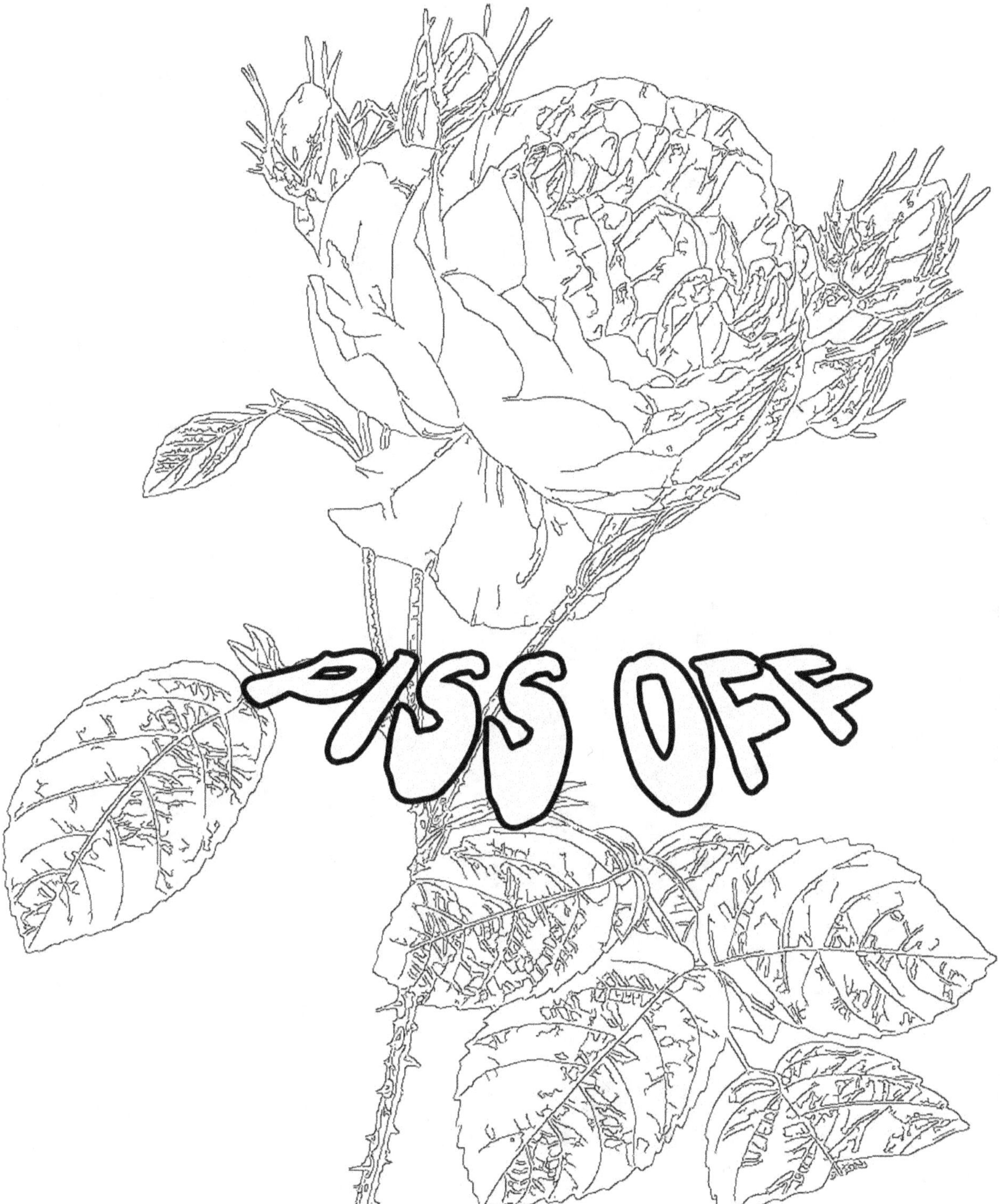
PISS OFF

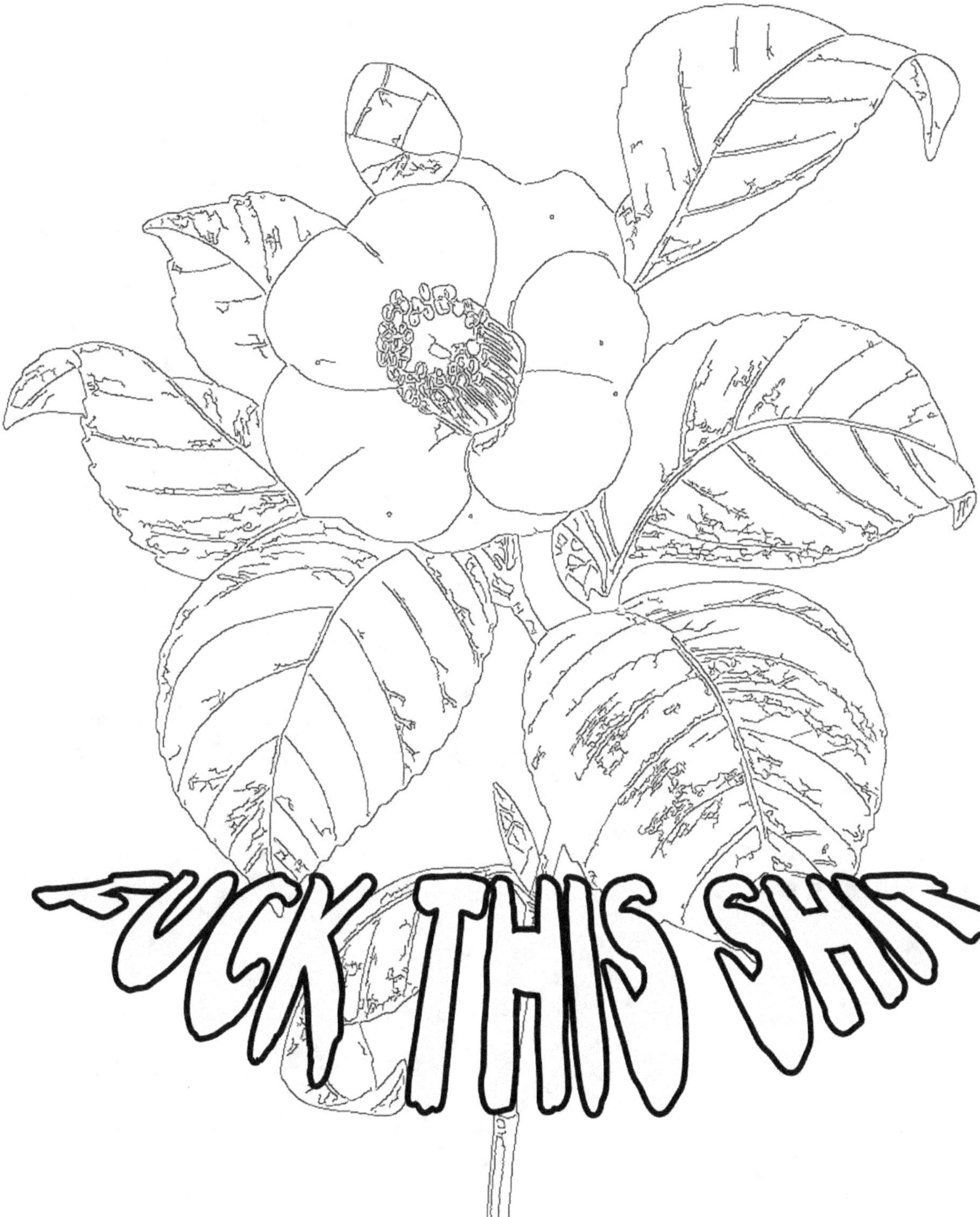
FUCK THIS SHIT

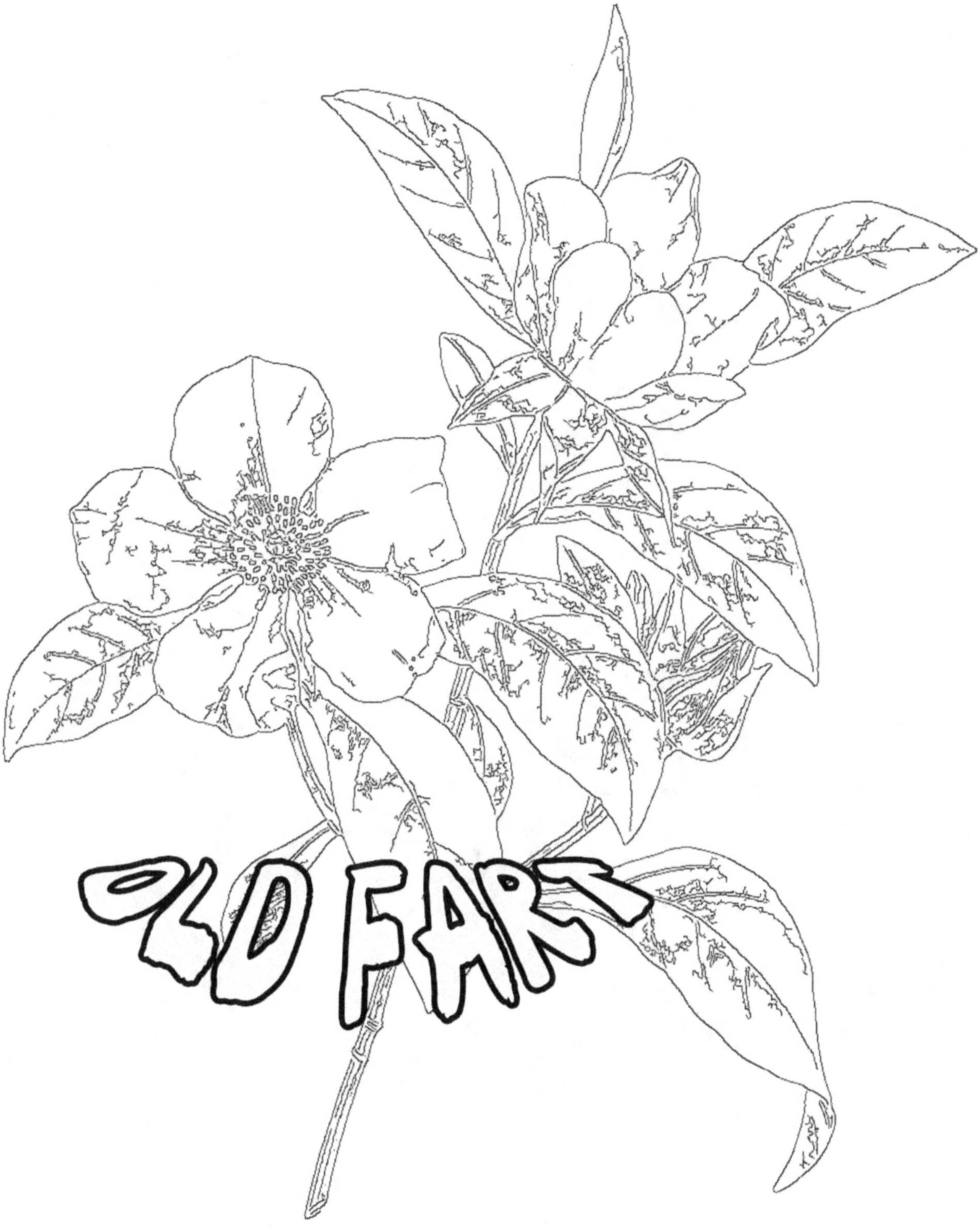
OLD FART

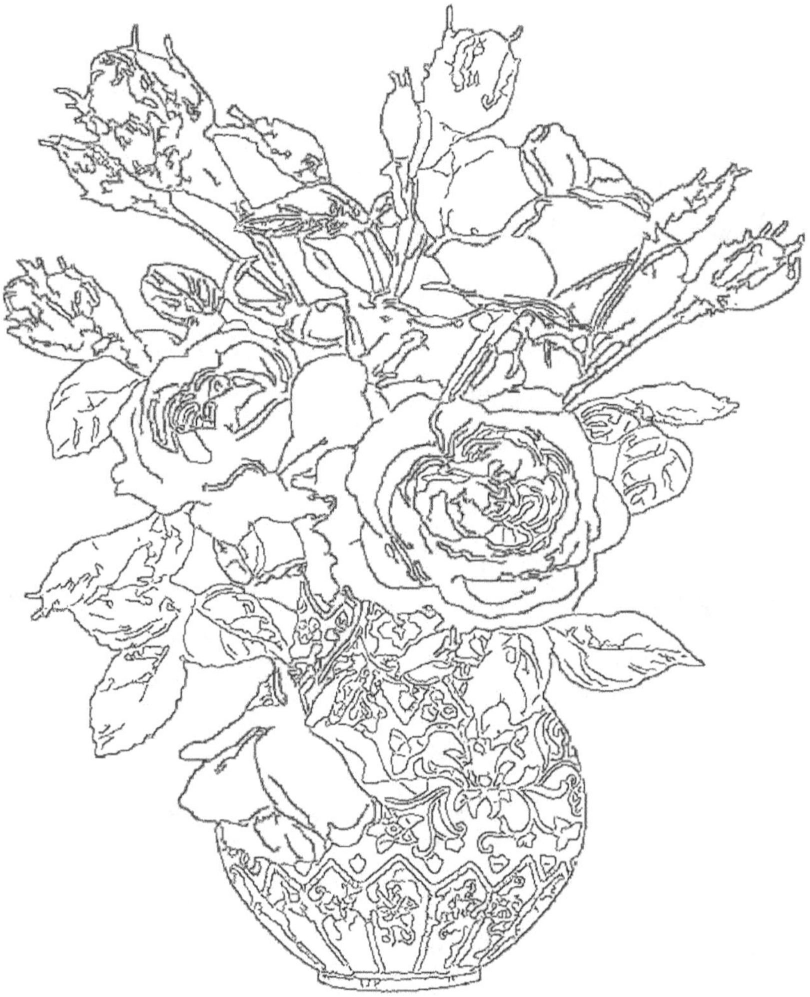

Have a good day.

www.ingramcontent.com/pod-product-compliance
Lightning Source LLC
Chambersburg PA
CBHW081619220526
45468CB00010B/2943